D1539272

The Caribou

The *Caribou*

By Lorle K. Harris

DILLON PRESS, INC.
Minneapolis, Minnesota 55415

Photographic Acknowledgments

The photographs are reproduced through the courtesy of the Alaska Division of Tourism, Rod Allin/Tom Stack & Associates, Tim Christie, Bob Firth/ Firth Photo Bank, A. Murie/Jan O. Murie, Al Nelson/Tom Stack & Associates, Mark Newman/Tom Stack & Associates, Leonard Lee Rue III, John Sarvis/ U.S. Fish and Wildlife Service, and Tom Stack/Tom Stack & Associates.

Library of Congress Cataloging-in-Publication Data

Harris, Lorle.
The caribou / by Lorle K. Harris.
(A Dillon remarkable animals book)
Includes index.
Summary: Examines the appearance, habitat, and behavior of the caribou, discusses its relationship with humans, and describes a year in the life of one individiaul caribou.
ISBN 0-87518-391-3
1. Caribou—Juvenile literature. [1. Caribou.] I. Title. II. Series.
QL737.U55H369   1988
599.73'57—dc 19   88-18953
                                                                    CIP
                                                                    AC

Dillon Press, Inc., 242 Portland Avenue South
Minneapolis, Minnesota 55415

Printed in the United States of America
1 2 3 4 5 6 7 8 9 10 97 96 95 94 93 92 91 90 89 88

Contents

Facts about the Caribou 6

1. A Splendid Animal 9

2. Adapting to the Arctic 21

3. Enemies of the Caribou 31

4. A Year in the Life of a Caribou 43

Glossary 56

Index 59

Facts about the Caribou

Scientific Name: *Rangifer tarandus*

Varieties: Barren-ground caribou, woodland caribou, Peary's caribou, reindeer, cross-breeds

Range: Throughout the arctic and subarctic regions of North America, Scandinavia, and Asia

Description:

Length—6 to 8 feet (1.8 to 2.4 meters) for male; female is smaller

Height—4 to 5 feet (1.2 to 1.5 meters) for male; female is smaller

Weight—250 to 700 pounds (113 to 318 kilograms) for male; female is lighter

Physical Features—Broad hoofs which support it in snow; many-pointed antlers which are used against enemies and rival males; keen sense of smell; four-chamber stomach for storing food as cud

Color—Medium-brown coat with white neck; male has a white mane around the throat

Distinctive Habits: Migrates hundreds of miles each year (except woodland and Peary's caribou); when surprised by enemies, rears up and releases an alarm scent from glands in its hoofs; each year sheds antlers and begins to grow a new pair; female returns every year to give birth in the same calving ground where it was born

Food: Sedges, grasses, dwarf birch, mushrooms, lichens

Reproductive Cycle: Pairs mate for one year only; female gives birth to one calf in June and raises it alone

Chapter 1

A Splendid Animal

Summer comes late and leaves early in the land of the barren-ground caribou. The sun still shines at midnight during the few weeks of arctic summer. It provides enough sunlight for the growth of grasses and small plants that cling to the ground, but not for trees. This great treeless plain is called the barren lands, or the **tundra.***

The tundra stretches across the most northern parts of North America, Scandinavia, and the Soviet Union. To the north, the tundra reaches the Arctic Ocean and meets the ice that covers the North Pole. To the south, forests of scrubby spruce grow where the year-round hours of sunlight are longer.

The caribou and their cousins, the reindeer of

*Words in **bold type** are explained in the glossary at the end of this book.

The smaller and light-colored reindeer live on the tundra of Asia and Scandinavia.

Scandinavia and Siberia, have lived in the Arctic for thousands of years. Caribou probably came to North America across the land bridge that joined Asia to Alaska thousands of years ago. They spread through the continent as far south as what are now the states bordering Canada, from Washington to Maine.

The Deer Family

Caribou are members of the deer family. Other **species**, or kinds, of deer include the mule deer of the western United States, the white-tailed deer of the east and southeast, elk, and moose. As members of the deer family, caribou are **cud** chewers, or **ruminants**. Instead of upper front teeth, they have a hard pad in the upper jaw. They press food up against this pad to break the food up into small pieces before swallowing it. The stomach is divided into four parts, each with a special job to do. The first part stores and softens the food, and later returns it to the mouth as cud to be chewed again. Later, the other parts mix the cud with stomach juices to help digest it.

Like all deer, caribou have **antlers**. Unlike other deer, however, both male and female caribou grow antlers. Antlers appear when a caribou calf is a month old. At first they look like little buttons. By the time a calf is four months old, they have grown into small spikes. At the age of six months, a male's spikes are already 10 inches (25 centimeters) long, and those of a female 6 inches (15 centimeters) long.

As the antlers grow, they are covered by a smooth, hairy skin called **velvet**. Blood vessels in the velvet carry the food that the antlers need to grow through the spring and early summer. Late in summer, the caribou shed their velvet to reveal magnificent, gleaming racks of antlers.

Antlers are important to the caribou. They use their antlers to attack enemies such as the wolf or grizzly bear. And the males lock antlers with rivals as they fight for the right to mate. They shed their antlers every year after the mating season is over. The females keep theirs until after the birth of their babies the following spring.

Unlike the hoofs of deer, the caribou's hoofs are built to plow through snow. The two front toes of its hoof and the **dewclaw**, or imperfect

Hairy velvet covers the growing antlers throughout the spring and summer.

toe, above the heel spread its weight when it stands and keeps the caribou from sinking deep into the snow. The rounded edges of its hoofs shrink and harden in the winter to prevent slipping on ice and snow. The edges also help the caribou to dig through crusty snow to find food.

Varieties of Caribou

Scientists divide the caribou into four main varieties, or groups: barren-ground caribou, woodland caribou, Peary's caribou, and reindeer. Mixing between varieties is common where territories or **migration** routes meet or overlap. When members of different varieties mate, their offspring (calves) often look like one variety, but act like another.

The caribou also have scientific names. Scientists have assigned Latin names to plants and animals to identify them for other scientists all over the world. To scientists, the barren-ground caribou is *Rangifer tarandus groenlandicus.* To other

Barren-ground caribou bulls feed on the tundra. One bull rests, watching for predators.

English-speaking people, it is simply known by its common name, barren-ground caribou.

The bull (male) is a splendid animal. He stands over 4 feet (1.2 meters) tall at the shoulder and may weigh more than 350 pounds (158 kilograms). His widespread antlers may measure 5 feet (1.5 meters) across. A band of white around his neck, which becomes a mane below his throat, sets off his cinnamon-brown coat. His coloring blends well with the scattered rocks and blowing snow of the tundra and makes it hard for his enemies to see him.

The cow (female) caribou, slightly smaller than the male, has the same coloring, but no mane. Her antlers are smaller and have fewer points than those of the male.

The barren-ground caribou are constantly on the move across the open plains of the North American tundra. In **herds** of thousands they travel between winter and summer ranges. They often cover as much as 400 miles (644 kilometers) on their journeys. Nothing stands in their way as they migrate north in the spring and south in the fall. They trot through ice fields, wade through marshes, swim swollen rivers, and climb mountains. They walk, stop, feed quickly, and move on. If the weather is stormy or the food supply scant, they change their route.

The woodland caribou, *Rangifer tarandus caribou*, once ranged along the border between the United States and Canada from Maine to Washington. There are now fewer than 2,000 left. They live mainly in the Canadian provinces of British Columbia, Ontario, Manitoba, Newfoundland, and in northern Idaho. Since they prefer higher elevations, the woodland caribou are often found in the mountains. They feed on a kind of **lichen** that hangs from the trees.

The pale, almost white Peary's caribou, *Rangifer tarandus pearyi*, live in wooded areas of the arctic islands in the far north. Unlike the large, husky woodland caribou with their heavy antlers, Peary's caribou are much smaller and their antlers lighter.

Reindeer, *Rangifer tarandus tarandus*, live on the barren grounds of Scandinavia and the Siberian tundra of the Soviet Union. Under 4 feet (1.2 meters) in height, they are smaller and lighter in color than the North American caribou.

Above: Peary's caribou are small and have light antlers. *Left:* A woodland caribou cow stands in a forest in Canada. The cow has shed her antlers and is growing a new one.

Like other animals, the caribou must struggle for survival. Yet over thousands of years, they have changed in unusual ways that have allowed them to thrive in the snowy lands of the north.

Chapter 2

Adapting to the Arctic

The barren-ground caribou could not change the icy climate of its homeland, so it adjusted to its arctic **habitat**. This process is called **adaptation**. The caribou's adaptation to the harsh climate in which it lives is seen in every part of its life.

Its strong and tough body is made for life in the Arctic. A heavy outer coat of long, brittle guard hairs over a thick layer of fine, curly hair keeps the caribou warm and dry. Thick fur protects its **muzzle** as it sniffs out and digs for food beneath the snow.

The **circulation**, or movement, of the caribou's blood through its body keeps its temperature steady. The temperature of the upper body stays a warm 103°F (39°C). Yet the temperature

The barren-ground caribou bull has broad, heavy antlers, and a white mane around the throat.

of its legs and hoofs remains a much lower 50°F (10°C). Because the legs and hoofs can function at such low temperatures, the caribou does not have to use as much energy to keep warm.

The caribou has adapted well to the limited food supply of the winter tundra. Although few other plant-eating animals can find enough to eat during the arctic winter, the caribou's system allows it to survive on a diet of lichens and other small plants. The caribou also saves energy in winter by not traveling as far as in warmer times of the year. In addition, the caribou never over-grazes in any one area. Its feeding habits allow the plants to continue to grow and feed the caribou year after year.

Cows and Calves

The caribou's choice of birthplace, or calving ground, is also an adaptation to its habitat. For the barren-ground caribou, the calving grounds are on higher land than the winter range. There

A caribou calf huddles in the snow to avoid the chilling arctic wind.

spring snowstorms are more likely than rain. A rain-soaked coat gives no protection from an icy wind and could bring death to a baby caribou. However, snow mixed with air forms a blanket to protect the newborn calves from windchill.

At the calving ground, the caribou are also safe from their worst enemies, the wolves. At this time, the wolves are in the lowlands, busy digging dens for their pups. The open spaces of the tundra provide few hillsides suitable for a den, making the tundra safer for the caribou to give birth to their own young.

The wolf is also the worst enemy of the woodland caribou. In Ontario and Manitoba, the cows swim to islands far from shore where they will be safe from wolves when they give birth. They stay on the islands until their calves are strong enough to travel.

All the barren-ground calves are born in a period of two weeks early in June. This gives them the chance to grow in size and strength while the weather is warm and food is plentiful.

Caribou calves grow at a rapid rate. Almost as soon as a calf is born, it can stand, and in two or three days it can easily outrun a person. The calf doubles in size in less than two weeks. This ability to develop quickly gives the calf a better chance to survive in its harsh arctic habitat.

Wolves hunt caribou year-round, leaving them only long enough to raise their own young.

A caribou crosses a swollen river. Weak caribou, such as young calves, may not survive such river crossings.

Life and Death

Even so, only half of the calves live through the first year. Once they have left the calving grounds, wolves are constantly watching for young caribou separated from the herd. Many calves drown as they try to cross swiftly flowing rivers.

The insects that attack the caribou in summer may also bring death to the young animals. Warble flies and mosquitoes weaken the calves by sucking large amounts of blood. The nose-bot fly places its **larvae**, or newly hatched young, in the caribou's nose. The larvae then move to the throat. There they continue to grow, making it difficult, then impossible, for the caribou to breathe.

Although the caribou has little defense against these insects, it has developed ways of defending against other **predators**. A caribou may warn the herd of danger by crouching slightly with its head up and ears pointing forward. It wags its tail and holds one hind leg out to one side.

When surprised by an enemy, the caribou rears up and may run a short distance on its hind legs before galloping away. This dramatic warning signal is called an "excitation leap." Since the caribou's sense of smell is much keener than its eyesight, the caribou also uses scent as a danger

Their adaptations to the harsh arctic climate have made the barren-ground caribou well suited to life on the tundra.

signal. **Glands** in the caribou's upraised hoofs release an **alarm scent** which stays in the air for some time after the caribou has fled. Other migrating caribou that follow later will smell the alarm scent and flee the area of danger.

A Remarkable Animal

In producing barren-ground caribou, nature has made a truly remarkable animal. Without the skills to build shelters, their bodies have adapted well to the cold climate. They have developed defenses against their enemies. And they can travel great distances on their own strength.

Chapter 3

Enemies of the Caribou

Thousands of barren-ground caribou roam the far northern parts of Alaska and northern Canada and as far east as Greenland. They travel so closely bunched together that their antlers look like a moving forest.

Scientists have divided the barren-ground caribou into twelve main herds according to their calving grounds. The calving ground of the McKinley herd is near Mount McKinley in Alaska, and the Porcupine herd's calving ground lies not far from the Porcupine River of the Yukon Territory in Canada.

Scientists have learned that the size of caribou herds varies greatly from year to year. They think that, over periods of several years, the

Large herds of barren-ground caribou—some numbering in the thousands—migrate between ranges.

numbers of caribou do not change much unless people kill too many of the animals. They believe the food supply keeps the number of animals down to what their range can support.

Arctic Predators

Wolves also keep the caribou herds from becoming too large. Wolf packs follow the caribou wherever they go. When caribou gather in large groups during the end of winter and in early spring, wolves find hunting easy. They dash into a herd, scattering the caribou. In this way they find the slow-moving animals—cows heavy with unborn calves, old bulls, and young calves—and cut them off from the rest of the herd.

Wolves are not the only predators the caribou fear. Foxes, lynx, and grizzly bears also attack the caribou. Eagles swoop down on young calves.

No predators cause the caribou more misery than mosquitoes and other insects. Mosquitoes can suck a quart of blood each week from a single

During warmer months, caribou sometimes stand in cold patches of snow to avoid insects.

animal. Hundreds burrow into the caribou's noses and ears. They cluster in and around their eyes. The desperate caribou head into the wind to try to rid themselves of the pests. At times insects drive the caribou wild, causing them to stampede. Only the return of cold weather brings relief.

Human Enemies

Unfortunately for the caribou, their most dangerous enemy knows no season. Human hunters present a growing threat to the survival of the caribou. At the end of the last century, white people from areas to the south began moving into the Arctic to hunt wild game, including caribou. In Alaska, big game hunters with powerful guns killed many arctic animals for sport. The native people depended upon these animals for food, clothing, and shelter.

The big game hunters killed so many animals that some people feared the native Alaskans would not be able to get enough food. Concerned missionaries who worked with the native peoples brought reindeer to Alaska to replace some of the animals the hunters were taking. Some of the reindeer joined Alaskan caribou herds and lived in the wild. The native people raised others, much as ranchers in the American West raise cattle. By 1978 there were about 30,000 reindeer in Alaska.

Hunting wild caribou continued at a rapid pace with the coming of airplanes and snowmobiles. These modern machines made it easier for both white and native hunters to kill many caribou. From an airplane, a pilot could spot a herd and radio the information to hunting parties. Then the hunters would hop on their snowmobiles and chase the herd. Between 1965 and 1975, Alaska lost more than half of its caribou because of such hunting methods.

The Alaska Department of Fish and Game realized that the caribou would disappear entirely unless they took action. To give the animals a chance to recover, the department limited or completely stopped the hunting of several herds. Officials encouraged people to hunt wolves instead. Fortunately, the caribou started wintering farther from human settlements. At the same time, diseases killed many wolves.

Canada has found it harder to control hunting in the Northwest Territories. There are not

enough officials to enforce hunting laws, and Canadian Indians protest every effort to limit their hunting. They eat caribou meat and use the hides for clothing and shelter. Centuries-old customs are hard to change.

Humans threaten the caribou in other ways, too. As people bring modern ways to the Arctic, they leave behind oil spills and dumps of poisonous materials. Often no one knows or cares about the damage this waste may cause to the fragile tundra and the life it supports.

Attempts to Aid the Caribou

Even in places where engineers have tried to meet the needs of wildlife, animals have not responded well to their attempts to help. The Alaska pipeline crosses Alaska from Prudhoe Bay on the Arctic Ocean to Prince William Sound on the Pacific. Even though the pipeline has ramps and underpasses for wildlife, the caribou do not use them. They walk by, looking for a way

Snowmobiles have made it easier for native hunters to kill caribou on the tundra.

In many places across Alaska, the Alaska pipeline presents a barrier to caribou and other wildlife.

around the pipeline, and finally turn back. After several years, the barrier may force the caribou to change their migration route.

Hydro-Quebec, a Canadian power company, built a dam on the Caniapiscau River, 275 miles (443 kilometers) upstream from a caribou crossing at Limestone Falls. In 1984 the river ran very high at the time of the caribou migration. To make it easier for the caribou to cross the river, the company cut down on the amount of water allowed to flow from the dam. But instead of crossing closer to the dam where the flow was less, 4,000 to 5,000 caribou drowned as they were swept over the falls. A habit hundreds of years old ruled their migration. To them, Limestone Falls was the place to cross the river.

The woodland caribou of the Selkirk Mountains are also fighting for survival. A small herd moves through the mountains of southeastern British Columbia in Canada, northern Idaho, and northeastern Washington. Forest fires and heavy logging, as well as the loss of trees that are killed by spruce-bark beetles, cut down the size of the range needed by the caribou.

Another threat to the herd is the main east-west highway that cuts through the middle of their range. Highway crews put salt on the road in winter to melt the snow and ice. Attracted by

Woodland caribou are threatened by the loss of their forest habitat and by highways that bring hunters deeper into their ranges.

the salt, the caribou move onto the highway and are killed or injured by passing cars. The highway also brings in hunters who kill the animals unlawfully.

Fortunately, the Idaho Department of Fish and Game is not ready to give up its efforts to save the caribou. It hopes to increase the Selkirk herd by importing caribou from British Columbia over the next several years.

The people of Maine are attempting to bring woodland caribou back to their state. The Caribou Transport Corporation is raising a herd in captivity from a group of 27 caribou brought to Maine from Newfoundland. They hope to have enough animals in five years to release a small herd into the wild.

From their experiences with the caribou, people are learning that they must take responsibility for their actions in the wild. The United States and Canada now have laws to protect wild animals—the caribou and many others—that have been threatened by human actions. Instead of being the caribou's most feared enemies, humans are becoming their most helpful friends.

Chapter 4

A Year in the Life of a Caribou

It is early June. Pools of melting snow dot the tundra, and the wind blows constantly. In the shelter of a rocky ridge, a newborn barren-ground caribou rises shakily to his feet. The little male searches for his mother's **udder** and begins to nurse, but only for a few seconds. Then the reddish brown calf lies down again to rest.

After a few hours the mother rises and moves away. Turning to face the calf, she lowers her head and bobs it up and down, grunting at the same time. Her calf understands her message. He gets up and goes to his mother. Once more he nurses briefly. When she moves on, he follows.

After a while, the mother stops at a cotton grass meadow and grazes. All around her, scat-

A caribou calf rests on the summer tundra.

tered over the broad calving grounds, cows and calves graze side by side. Within two weeks, all the cows in the herd will have given birth to this year's babies.

In the first few days after birth, the cow and calf get to know each other. No two animals smell, sound, or look alike. Once mother and calf recognize each other's scent, they learn to recognize each other's sounds. The cow grunts, and the calf responds by bleating. Learning to recognize each other by sight comes last.

The March Begins

The caribou do not remain long at the calving grounds. As mother and calf move north, other cows and their babies follow them. After a long, hard winter and march to the calving ground, the mother is very thin and her coat ragged. She stops often to graze. Her calf nuzzles up to her to see what she is eating. Just four days old, he has his first taste of cotton grass and **sedges**.

Led by the cow and her calf, the caribou continue on their journey. Every day the herd grows larger as adult males and yearlings (the calves born a year ago) join the band. A yearling approaches the mother and her calf. With a jab of her antlers, the protective mother chases the intruder away.

The caribou march on. They walk in single file, each animal stepping in the tracks of the one in front of it. In some places the path has cut deep ruts in the rock. The caribou's hoofs make loud clicking noises as they march, and the grunts of cows calling their calves fill the air.

The calf grows rapidly, doubling his weight in two weeks. He begins to notice the other young caribou in the herd. One day he dashes after a nearby calf. They chase each other at top speed, running away from the herd and leaping over the rocks. Suddenly, the calf stops. His mother is nowhere in sight. Frightened, he bleats for help and runs around in circles, not knowing where to

A band of caribou swims across a river during the migration to the summer range.

turn. His bleating and that of his playmate echo through the air.

His mother appears at the top of a ridge. When she calls, he races toward her.

Danger Along the Way

As the migration continues, the caribou come to a river. Large chunks of ice tumble along the fast-moving stream. The cow walks along the edge looking for a safe place to cross. She enters the water, hesitates, and backs up to the shore. She tries again and again. At last she plunges in, her calf by her side. The herd follows.

Swimming with head and shoulders above the surface of the water, the caribou crowd together, touching each other in the crush. The racing water tugs at the swimmers on the edge of the herd. The current catches the calf and carries him downstream. Desperately, he struggles to reach the shore which is piled high with ice floes. Clumsily pawing the ice, he manages to get a grip and scramble ashore. Ice-cold water drips from his fur as he joins his mother who has been pacing along the river bank. The swift current carries other calves away as their mothers watch. They never see them again.

The surviving caribou keep moving along their migration route as other bands join the herd. Soon the animals number in the thousands. The caribou cover as much as 15 miles (24 kilometers) a day. It is now July, and the arctic sun shines day and night. Mosquitoes have hatched and have begun their attacks. The caribou walk into the wind to escape them. At noon they rest in the highest, coldest places they can find, where there are fewer mosquitoes. The caribou lie down in groups in open spaces. They face in all directions, watching for wolves and other enemies.

Preparing for Winter

Before long, the caribou are on the march again. They walk steadily, stopping briefly to feed

During the summer, caribou shed their heavy winter coats and grow new racks of antlers.

on willow shoots, grass, sedges, and mushrooms. The calf eats plants now, too, and he seldom nurses anymore.

The cow's ribs no longer show as she puts on fat to help her through the winter. She sheds her shaggy old fur coat and grows a new one of thick, dark brown fur. The calf's coat also darkens to a

In the fall, caribou rub their grown antlers on branches and trunks of shrubs to scrape off the velvet.

brownish gray. The cow has lost her antlers and is growing a new set, while the calf's spikes grow steadily.

The frosts and snowstorms of August mark the beginning of fall on the tundra. With the welcome arrival of colder weather, the mosquitoes disappear. By early September caribou quicken their pace as the march to the winter range begins.

During the journey south, small groups join the one the cow is leading. The bulls frequently stop to rub their antlers on the rough branches and trunks of shrubs. With much scraping, they finally rub all the velvet off their antlers. Now many racks of polished antlers gleam in the autumn sunlight.

The calf stops to watch two bulls locking antlers. They crash their antlers together and shove, testing each other's strength. The bulls tire quickly and move on.

By mid-October, the fighting among the bulls reaches its peak. The calf watches two mighty bulls push and twist. They kick up chunks of frozen sod as they try to force each other to the ground. The calf sprints to one side, just barely out of their way.

At last one bull gives up the fight and walks away. The winner goes to the calf's mother and

Two rival bulls lock antlers in a contest to determine which one is stronger.

quickly mates with her. He moves on to mate with another cow.

The days grow shorter as the march to the winter range continues. With the coming of the long winter night, the snow grows deeper. The cow paws through the snow with the sharp edges of her front hoofs. She digs a wide, round hole, called a **crater**, to reach the lichens, the caribou's main food in winter. She feeds and moves on.

All winter long, hungry wolves shadow the caribou. Many weaker caribou are taken, but not the cow and her calf.

As the days grow longer in February, the caribou become restless, and begin their migration to the summer range. The pregnant cows and the calves are the first to leave. The calf stays close to his mother until she reaches the calving ground. Then the cow pushes him away, for her yearling is now old enough to take care of himself. She is about to give birth to a new calf.

The Future of the Caribou

And so the yearly **cycle** of the caribou continues as it has for thousands of years. Will the cycle continue in the future? At this time, that question is a difficult one to answer. People have made many changes in the caribou's habitat, and

hunters have killed great numbers of the animals. Yet people are beginning to understand that what happens to one species of living things affects others, including humans.

Scientists and wildlife officials continue to study the caribou's needs and take action to preserve its habitat. They are trying to make sure that the caribou will march across the tundra for another thousand years.

The barren-ground caribou—what does the future hold?

Glossary

adaptation (add-ap-TAY-shuhn)—the ability of animals (including human beings) and plants to adjust to changes in their environment

alarm scent—an odor given off by an animal to warn others of its kind of danger

antlers—the bony, branched growths on the heads of members of the deer family

circulation (sur-kyoo-LAY-shuhn)—the movement of the blood through blood vessels by the pumping action of the heart

crater—a wide, round hole dug in the snow by caribou to reach food

cud—the partly digested food which the stomach of certain animals returns to the mouth for further chewing

cycle—a series of events that takes place regularly over a certain period of time

dewclaw—an incomplete toe on the back of the caribou's hind foot

glands—organs that make materials needed by the body for special purposes, such as sweat

habitat—the area where a plant or animal naturally lives

herd—a group of animals using the same calving ground, and traveling and living together

larvae (LAHR-vay)—the young of an insect that look unlike the parent and that must change before becoming adults

lichen (LY-kehn)—a small, scaly plant that is a combination of algae and fungi and that grows on rocks and trees

migration—the process of moving with the change of seasons from one area or climate to another for feeding or breeding

muzzle—the front part of an animal's head, including its jaw and nose

predators (PREHD-uh-tuhrz)—animals that hunt other animals for food

ruminants (ROO-muh-nehnts)—animals that have four-chamber stomachs and that chew cud

sedge—a grass-like plant that grows on marshy land

species (SPEE-sheez)—distinct kinds of individual plants or animals that have common characteristics and share a common name

tundra—the land bordering the arctic ice cap and reaching south to the edge of the northern forests

udder—the milk-producing organ of mammals which is used to feed young offspring

velvet—the smooth, hairy covering of antlers which supplies nutrition for growth of the antlers

Index

adaptation, 19, 21-24, 27-29
airplanes, 35
alarm scent, 29
Alaska Department of Fish and
    Game, 35
Alaska pipeline, 37-38
antlers, 11-12, 15, 16, 17, 45,
    50, 51, 53
Arctic, the, 9-10, 16, 17, 21,
    34, 37, 43
barren grounds. *See* tundra
bleating, 44, 45-47
calves, 11-12, 14, 23, 24, 26-27,
    32, 43-53
calving grounds, 22-24, 31, 43-
    44, 53
caribou, varieties of: barren-
    ground, 9, 14-16, 17, 21-
    24, 29, 30, 31, 43; Peary's,
    14, 17; reindeer, 9-10, 14,
    17, 34; woodland, 14, 17,
    24, 39-41
Caribou Transport Corpora-
    tion, 41
circulation, 21-22

coat, 16, 21, 44, 49-50
cotton grass, 43, 44
crater, 52-53
cud, 11
deer, 11-14
dewclaw, 12-14
excitation leap, 27-29
glands, 29
habitat, 16, 17, 21-23, 24, 29,
    53, 55
highway, 39-40
hoofs, 12-14, 22, 29, 45, 52-53
hunters, 34-37, 40, 53-55
Hydro-Quebec, 38-39
Idaho Department of Fish and
    Game, 40-41
lichens, 17, 22, 53
mane, 15-16
mating, 12, 14, 51-52
migration, 14, 16, 29, 38, 39,
    45, 47, 48, 51, 53
mosquitoes, 27, 32-33, 48, 50
muzzle, 21
native Indians, 34, 35-37
nose-bot fly, 27

pollution, 37
predators: animal, 12, 23-24, 26, 32, 35, 48, 53; human, 34-37, 40, 41, 53-55; insect, 27, 32-33, 48, 50
protection laws, 35, 41
ranges, 16, 22, 39, 51, 53
Rangifer tarandus caribou (woodland), 17
Rangifer tarandus groenlandicus (barren-ground), 14
Rangifer tarandus pearyi (Peary's), 17
Rangifer tarandus tarandus (reindeer), 17

river crossings, 26, 38-39, 47-48
ruminants, 11
sedges, 44, 49
snowmobiles, 35
stampede, 33
stomach, 11
tundra, 9, 16, 17, 22, 24, 37, 43, 50, 55
udder, 43
velvet, 12, 51
warble flies, 27
wolves, 23-24, 26, 32, 35, 48, 53